Contents

The Viking world   6

Building materials   8

A Viking longhouse   10

Viking towns   12

Inside a Viking home   14

Viking families   16

Women's work   18

Life on the farm   20

Food and drink   22

Forges and workshops   24

Games and pastimes   26

Timeline   28

Glossary   29

Index and resources   30

Words in **bold** can be found
in the glossary.

The Viking world

The Vikings came from Scandinavia, the region of northern Europe that is made up of modern-day Denmark, Norway and Sweden. From the 8th to the 11th centuries, many Vikings left Scandinavia on journeys of piracy, exploration and **commerce**. This time is often called the 'Viking Age'.

↑ In this 19th century drawing the artist has imagined what a Viking raid might have looked like.

Farmers

The people of Scandinavia were farmers and fishers, who lived on small farms. Some of these farms were clustered in small villages, while others lay far from their nearest neighbours. While most Scandinavians stayed at home, some set out on exciting voyages. The voyagers were called Vikings, which means 'pirate', or 'piracy' in the **Old Norse** language.

Viking Life

HOMES

Nicola Barber

First published in 2010 by Wayland

Copyright © Wayland 2010

Wayland
338 Euston Road
London NW1 3BH

Wayland Australia
Level 17/207 Kent Street
Sydney NSW 2000

Series Editor: Nicola Edwards
Series Consultant: Annette Trolle
Designer: Jane Hawkins
Picture Researcher: Kathy Lockley

British Library Cataloguing in Publication Data
Barber, Nicola.
Viking life.
  Homes.
  1. Vikings--Dwellings--Juvenile literature. 2. Vikings--
  Social life and customs--Juvenile literature.
  I. Title
  392.3'6'089395-dc22

ISBN: 978 0 7502 6383 2

Picture acknowledgements
akg-images: 12; akg-images/Erich Lessing/Statens Historiska Museum,Stockholm: 15, 29;
The Art Gallery Collection/Alamy: 9; YvetteCardozo/Alamy: 18; Werner Forman Archive/National
Museum of Denmark,Copenhagen: Cover (inset), 25, 28; Werner Forman Archive/Statens
HistoriskaMuseum, Stockholm: 5, 17; Werner Forman Archive/Universitetets Oldsaksamling, Oslo:
24; Rolf Hicker Photography/Alamy: Title page, 16; Ian Thompson, courtesy hurstwic.org: 11; Icelandic
Photo Agency/Alamy: 10; iStockphoto 20; Ladi Kim/Alamy: 23; LOOK Die Bildagentur der Fotografen
GmbH/Alamy: 19B; Esben Schlosser Mauritsen: Cover (main), 8; Musée dela Tapisserie, Bayeux,
France/With special authorisation of the city of Bayeux/Giraudon/Bridgeman Art Library, London: 21;
North Wind PicturesArchives/akg-images: 6; Pixonnet.com/Alamy: 22; Ted Spiegel/Corbis: 13;
Glyn Thomas/Alamy: 7; Tim Thompson/Corbis: 14; © York Archaeological Trust: 4, 26, 27

The author and publisher would like to thank Torkild Waagaard for his kind permission to reproduce his
artwork of a Viking helmet on the panels in thisbook.

Printed in China

Wayland is a division of Hachette Children's Books, an Hachette UK company.

www.hachette.co.uk

Sailors and settlers

The Vikings were superb sailors. They used their skills to sail across seas, **raiding** and **plundering** as they went. Vikings from different parts of Scandinavia travelled in different directions. The Vikings from Norway set out westwards on voyages across the North Sea. The Danish Vikings also sailed west. Meanwhile, the Swedish Vikings set off eastwards along rivers, on trading expeditions that took them deep into the European continent.

Many of these Vikings built settlements outside Scandinavia. Some were temporary camps put up by raiding expeditions to wait out the winter months. Others were more permanent, for example the Viking settlements at York (Jorvik) in England, or Dubh-Linn (Dublin) in Ireland. Although the buildings have long gone, we know about Viking settlements from evidence uncovered by **archaeologists** in these places.

➡

Snorri Sturluson lived after the end of the Viking Age, but he wrote about the Vikings and their beliefs.

Snorri Sturluson 1179 CE – 1241 CE

Snorri Sturluson was an Icelandic poet and politician. In 1206 he settled at a farmhouse in Reykholt, Iceland. It was here that he wrote his most famous works including the Prose (or Younger) Edda (about Old Norse myths) and a history of the Norwegian kings. At Reykholt Snorri built a bathhouse with a hot pool for bathing. The water was heated naturally by hot, volcanic rocks just below the surface of the earth. After disagreement with the king of Norway, Snorri was murdered at Reykholt in 1241.

Building materials

In many parts of Scandinavia there were large forests, so the Vikings made use of the trees to build wooden houses. In other places where timber was not so plentiful, they used other materials including stone and thick layers of **turf**.

Wooden houses

In Scandinavia, a typical Viking farm was centred around a large building called a **longhouse**. This was a long, low building made out of timber logs or planks, with a steep, pointed roof. The roof of a longhouse could be covered with thatch, wooden tiles or layers of bark topped with turf. There were no windows, but some houses had small holes cut into the wooden walls or into the roof, possibly with shutters. There was a hole in the roof to allow smoke to escape from the fire on the hearth below. Most houses did not have chimneys.

A reconstructed Viking longhouse at the Viking fortress Fyrkat in Denmark. Large houses like this were owned by kings and chieftains.

8

↑ The wood in this picture is being prepared to build longships.

In Viking towns and elsewhere, some wooden houses were covered with wattle and daub. A wattle is a panel of interweaved branches that is smeared with daub – mud or cow dung – to make a waterproof surface.

A Viking Object

This scene from the Bayeux Tapestry (see page 21) shows the kinds of tools used by the Vikings for woodwork. Different types of axes were used to chop down trees, to trim the branches off, and to split the timber into pieces. The man on the right-hand side of the picture is using a T-shaped axe to shape the timber into planks.

Stone and turf

In the 800s the Vikings began to settle in places such as the Orkney and Shetland islands, and in Iceland (from the 870s). Without a ready supply of timber they had to use other materials for building. They built foundations and walls out of stones. Blocks of turf (grass with soil held in the roots) were cut out of the ground, watered thoroughly then allowed to dry. These turf 'bricks' were laid on top of each other to build walls and roofs. Inside, precious timber was used for supports to hold the roof up, and wooden panels along the walls helped to keep out the cold and damp.

A Viking longhouse

The longhouse was the centre of a Viking farm.
It was often surrounded by outbuildings, and
the whole farm was protected by a fence or wall.
In some places, six to eight farms were built close
together to create a small village.

A reconstruction of a longhouse at
Stong in Iceland. The main hall is
just over 12 metres long.

Animals and people

At the beginning of the Viking Age, a longhouse contained all the **livestock**
and people on a farm. The animal stalls were inside the longhouse next to
the human living quarters. Later, the livestock were moved to separate
barns, and hay for winter feed was stored in **byres**.

Inside a longhouse

Typically, a longhouse was between 5 and 7 metres wide, and up to
30 metres long, depending on the wealth and importance of the owner.
Inside there was a long room with a hard-earth floor. A fire burned on
a central hearth made from stone.

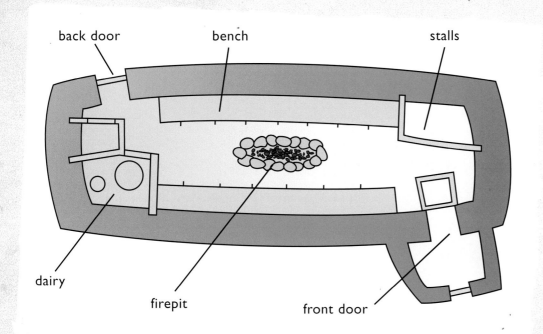

back door   bench   stalls

dairy   firepit   front door

This plan shows the layout of a longhouse. The fire is in the centre with long benches running down either side of the main hall.

The fire was needed for heat and light, and for cooking. The air inside a longhouse was usually smoky as, without a chimney, the smoke simply drifted upwards to the smoke hole in the roof.

The main room of a longhouse was where the people of the farm lived and slept. Some longhouses had extra rooms, for example a dairy or a room for spinning. Some even had a separate bedroom for the farmer and his wife. Outside there were small buildings for workshops and weaving sheds. They often had floors that were dug into the ground, with low roofs (called pit houses). Big farms had their own **forges** where iron was heated and shaped to make tools and other equipment (see pages 24-25).

Written at the time

This description of a longhouse, with small windows set into the roof, comes from *Njal's Saga*:

'Gunnar's hall was made all of wood, and roofed with beams above, and there were window-slits under the beams that carried the roof, and they were fitted with shutters… Gunnar slept in a loft above the hall, and so did Hallgerda and his mother.'

Viking towns

The Vikings were traders as well as raiders. As trade developed, towns such as Hedeby in Denmark (now in modern-day Germany), Birka in Sweden and Bergen in Norway became important and bustling centres.

Hedeby

Viking towns were often on a waterfront – either on the sea or a river – so that ships could load and unload their goods. Hedeby, for example, lay at the end of a sheltered **fjord** (deep inlet), which allowed ships to sail in from the Baltic Sea. These settlements were so important to the Viking kings that they were well protected against enemies. Both Hedeby and Birka were surrounded by **ramparts** made of earth. Inside the rampart at Hedeby, the houses were laid out in an orderly grid pattern. They were made from wood and wattle and daub.

 This artist's painting shows what Hedeby might have looked like in Viking times.

12

Jorvik

The Vikings also built towns, abroad. Archaeologists have uncovered a Viking settlement called Jorvik beneath present-day York in northeast England. There was already a settlement at York when the Vikings arrived in the 860s, but by 1000 Jorvik was a bustling town full of merchants and craftworkers.

Life in a town

Viking towns were fairly smelly and unhealthy places. All Viking settlements had wells, for water, but. there were no systems of rubbish collection or drainage. Rubbish was thrown on the floor, while sewage was put into a pit called a **midden**, or dumped into holes dug in the ground. In Jorvik, archaeologists have discovered that the wooden houses were rebuilt every 20 years or so. Each time, the houses were built on a slightly higher level because of the amount of rubbish trodden into the floor.

Written at the time

The Arab traveller Ibrahim Al-Tartushi came from Cordoba in Spain, which at the time was a much wealthier place than Hedeby. On his visit to Hedeby he noticed some unusual features of the town and its people:

'[Hedeby] is a very large town at the extreme end of the world ocean... The town is poor in goods and riches. People eat mainly fish which exist in abundance... The right to divorce belongs to the women... Artificial eye make-up is another peculiarity; when they wear it their beauty never disappears, indeed it is enhanced in both men and women.'

 Some Viking houses have been reconstructed at Hedeby.

Inside a Viking home

Without windows the inside of a Viking home was usually quite dark. The only natural light came through the smoke hole in the roof.

Light

The Vikings relied on the fire for light, and on small lamps. These lamps were made out of stones that were carved into dish shapes and filled with oil. The oil came from fish or seals, and the wick for the lamp was usually made from **cottongrass**.

Furniture

There was much less furniture in a Viking house than you would find in a modern home. In a longhouse there were ledges made out of earth built in along the walls. These were used for sitting and working during the day, and for sleeping at night. Precious possessions such as jewellery or money were locked in a large wooden chest.

⬆ You can see the bench built along the wall inside this reconstruction of a longhouse.

Some wealthy Viking homes had beautifully carved beds for the master and mistress, as well as wall hangings or wooden carvings along the walls to keep out draughts.

Comfort and cleanliness

The Vikings made mattresses that were stuffed with straw. They slept between sheepskins or wool blankets to keep warm. Some even had snug quilts and pillows filled with feathers or down. In Iceland, some longhouses had separate bathhouses. They made use of the hot water that comes directly from the ground in many places in Iceland. This water is heated by volcanic activity near to the earth's surface.

A Viking Object

Most Viking homes had a wooden chest. These items of furniture were useful for storing valuable belongings, and for sitting on. Some were quite plain. Others, like the one shown here, were highly decorated with ironwork.

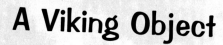

Viking families

There was very little privacy in a Viking home. Generations of families lived, ate and slept together in the same space.

Modern-day people re-enact life in Viking times at L'Anse aux Meadows in North America.

Family loyalties

The father was the head of a Viking family, but when the men were away raiding, fishing or hunting, the women ran the household and the farm. When a man died, his eldest son inherited the farm. Any younger sons had to find other land to farm. There was very strong loyalty between family members. If one member of a family was harmed, the others would seek revenge. This led to many **feuds** between rival families.

Although it was the Viking men who went raiding, not all women and children stayed at home. Many Viking families set off on perilous sea voyages to make new homes in places such as Iceland, Greenland and even North America.

Women

Women had a lot of independence in Viking society. When a girl got married she took with her a **dowry**. This could include cloth, a spinning wheel, and even jewellery and farm animals. Her dowry remained her personal property, and became part of her inheritance to her children after her death. If a husband mistreated his wife, or was lazy, she could divorce him.

Thralls

Most farmers hired workers and servants to work on the farm in exchange for food, lodging and wages. Farmers also had slaves, called **thralls**. Many thralls were people from outside Scandinavia who had been captured during raids or battles. They worked alongside the other farmworkers, but they were often given the hardest and dirtiest jobs.

A Viking Object

This pendant provides us with some evidence of what Viking women looked like. The woman's long hair is tied back in a bun, and her dress has a long train that sweeps behind. In her hands she carries a drinking horn. She may be a Valkyrie, a figure from Norse myths. The Vikings believed that in the afterlife the Valkyries searched out and welcomed dead warriors into Valhalla, the 'hall of heroes'.

⬆ This silver pendant comes from Birka in Sweden.

Women's work

Viking women were in charge of running the household and, if the men were away, the farm too. Wealthy Vikings had servants and thralls to help them carry out their daily tasks.

Looking after the household

It was up to a Viking woman to make sure that everyone in her household was fed and clothed. She prepared food every day, and she also had to make sure that there was enough food to last through the long winter months (see pages 22 to 23 for more about food and drink). Women cared for anyone in the household who was sick, using plants and **herbs** to make medicines as well as treating injuries and wounds.

Modern-day women re-enact preparations for a Viking feast in Norway. A cauldron hangs over the fire for cooking.

Unn the Deep-Minded
834 CE – 900 CE

The story of Unn the Deep-Minded takes up the early parts of the Laxdaela Saga (written around 1245). It shows just how independent and powerful Viking women could be. Unn was a widow who left Norway for Scotland with her son Thorstein. When Thorstein was killed in battle, Unn decided to join the rest of her family in Iceland. She ordered a ship to be built, and once in Iceland claimed land and built a farm, which she ran herself until her death.

Spinning and weaving

Making cloth for clothing as well as essential items such as ship's sails was an important part of day-to-day activity. Clothing was made from wool and linen. Sheep's **fleeces** had to be cleaned then combed before the wool could be spun into thread. Linen was made from fibres in the stem of the flax plant. The women wove the threads into cloth on a **loom**. Woollen cloth was often dyed, using various plants to create different colours. Then the cloth was cut and sewn. Linen was mostly used for undergarments, as it was less scratchy than wool!

A modern-day Viking woman prepares food in a reconstructed longhouse in Greenland, near to where Erik the Red once lived.

Life on the farm

Viking farmers kept livestock, most importantly cattle and sheep. Depending on where they lived, they also grew crops such as barley, rye and oats.

↑ Descendants of the sturdy ponies the Vikings used for riding and carrying loads can still be found on Iceland.

Feeding the animals

In many parts of the Viking world, particularly Norway, cattle and sheep were driven up to high pastures to feed on the lush grass during the summer. They were brought down again to fields near the longhouse for the winters. While sheep could mostly survive outside, cattle were kept in barns during the long winter months. Farmers grew hay, which they cut and stored to feed the animals while they were inside. If there was not enough hay to feed the whole herd, some cattle were killed at the beginning of the winter. The meat was salted, dried or smoked to preserve it (prevent it from going bad).

Many other animals, including goats, pigs and hens were kept on Viking farms. Horses were particularly important in Iceland. The Icelandic Vikings bred tough little ponies which they used for carrying loads and for riding.

Growing crops

In the spring, the Vikings prepared the ground for planting crops. They used a simple plough pulled by oxen to cut grooves in the soil. Animal manure was spread on the fields to keep the soils **fertile**. As well as barley, rye and oats, the Vikings grew wheat, flax for linen, and vegetables such as cabbages, onions and peas.

A Viking Object

The Bayeux Tapestry was made to record the conquest of England in 1066 by William, Duke of Normandy (William the Conqueror). The Normans were descended from Vikings who had settled in this part of France, so we can be fairly certain that the Normans used similar practices to the Vikings for farming. This scene shows a plough being pulled by a donkey. In fact, the Vikings would have used an ox or a pony for this work.

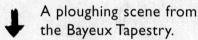

A ploughing scene from the Bayeux Tapestry.

Food and drink

The Vikings mostly ate food made from the animals they had raised, and the crops they had grown on their own farms. Added to this were fish, wild animals such as boar or deer, and wild fruits, herbs and honey.

Mealtimes

The Vikings ate two meals a day, one in the middle of the morning and one in the evening. The food was eaten off wooden plates, called trenchers, or out of wooden bowls. People used their knives to cut meat, and spoons made from horn or metal to eat stew or porridge – there were no forks.

↑ The Vikings had metal cauldrons to cook their food, and wooden plates and bowls to eat off.

Bread and dairy

Most bread was made from barley flour, and it was often quite coarse and gritty. The bread dough was kneaded in a big wooden trough before being baked on a flat pan held over the fire.

Bread being prepared at a Viking festival in Sweden.

Wealthy people who could afford it ate white bread made from sifted wheat flour.

The milk collected from cows and sheep was turned into butter, cheese and a type of sour milk called *skyr*. The *skyr* was stored in barrels which were half buried in the ground to keep them cool. In the winter, when there was no fresh milk, *skyr* was the only dairy product available on the farm.

Diet and drinks

People's diet depended on where in the Viking world they lived. Fish were important for people who lived near a coast or river. In the milder climate of Denmark more crops could be grown than in the highlands of Norway. All over the Viking world, however, ale made from barley was the main drink. Other drinks included milk, beer, wine and mead (made from honey).

Written at the time

These lines describing a Viking feast in a wealthy home come from the *Rigsthula*, part of the *Elder (Poetic) Edda*:

'Then took Mother a figured cloth,
white, of linen, and covered the board;
thereafter took she a fine-baked loaf,
white of wheat and covered the cloth:
next she brought forth plenteous dishes,
set with silver, and spread the board
with brown-fried bacon and roasted birds.
There was wine in a vessel and rich-
wrought goblets;
they drank and revelled while day
went by.'

Forges and workshops

A Viking farmer and his workers dealt with all the jobs that needed doing around the farm. Their work included making and mending tools and other equipment.

Working with metal

Most farms were equipped with a forge where iron could be heated and worked. The red-hot iron was beaten and shaped into tools such as axes, shears for cutting fleeces, ploughs, and **sickles** for harvesting crops, as well as nails, knives and weapons. There were also blacksmiths who travelled from one settlement to another. These craftworkers were skilled in making items such as sharp swords and spears, and were very highly respected. They also produced everyday objects such as keys and locks, or cauldrons for cooking.

⬆ A blacksmith (left) holds a piece of hot iron with tongs while he beats it with a hammer. The man on the right is using bellows to keep the fire hot. This carving comes from a church in Norway.

24

The blacksmiths themselves used special tools in the forge. Tongs were needed to hold the red-hot iron, and hammers for beating it. Shears were used to cut sheets of metal, and chisels and files for shaping nails.

Town workshops

In Viking towns, archaeologists have uncovered evidence of people carrying out many kinds of trade in houses that doubled as workshops. In Jorvik, for example, there were workshops where people made wooden bowls and cups, leather shoes, knives, jewellery, combs and tools of all description. Craftworkers used a wide range of metals to make jewellery, from gold and silver for the wealthy to cheaper metals such as copper and lead. Combs were a popular item, used to comb the hair and to get rid of head lice! They were made from animal bone or **antler**.

A Viking Object

These Viking keys are from Denmark. Keys were made from iron and bronze in the Viking Age. You can see how carefully these keys have been made and shaped by the blacksmith. The keys might have belonged to a Viking woman. Viking women looked after the household keys and carried them on belts around their waists.

Games and pastimes

During the long, dark winter evenings, the Vikings loved to play games and, most of all, tell stories. These stories, or sagas, were told from memory and passed down through the generations.

Skalds

The sagas tell tales of heroes, feuds, battles and the histories of the Scandinavian kings. Viking kings liked to be entertained by poets, called *skalds*. The *skalds* made up and performed poems that praised the king and his achievements. If the king liked the poem, he rewarded the *skald* well, for example with fine jewellery.

Board games

Other indoor entertainment included dice and board games. The Vikings played a board game called *hneftafl*, in which one player with a small number of pieces had to protect them against another player with a much larger number. We don't, however, know the exact rules for this popular game.

These gaming pieces and part of a **hneftafl** board were found at Jorvik.

Other board games were draughts and, later in the Viking Age, chess.

Outdoor entertainment

During the winter, the Vikings went skiing, sledging and skating. They made skates from animal bones tied on underneath their shoes. In the summer months, they raced their boats, swam and held wrestling matches. In Iceland, horse fights were very popular. The Vikings placed bets on the winner.

Hunting was popular, both for food and for fun. The Vikings hunted the animals that lived in the Scandinavian woods – such as bear, wolves, deer and wild boar. They used **falcons** (birds of prey) to hunt smaller animals such as hares, or small birds.

A Viking Object

This boot and skate were found in Jorvik. The leather boot is fastened by a wooden toggle. The skate is made from animal bone, and would have been tied on to the boot. In the past, the rivers that flow through York (Jorvik) often flooded and froze over during the winters. The Vikings used skates such as these to travel over the ice.

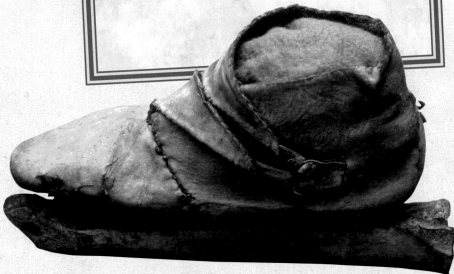

⬆ A leather boot and bone skate from Jorvik.

Timeline

CE

c.750s	Founding of Birka
789	Vikings raid southern England
793	Vikings raid monastery of Lindisfarne, Northumbria, England
795	Vikings raid monastery of St Columba on Iona, Scotland
800s	Vikings settle the Orkney and Shetland Islands
c.800	Founding of Hedeby
830s	Viking attacks on western Europe and Ireland begin
841	Vikings establish a longphort at Dubh-Linn (Dublin) in Ireland
843	Vikings plunder Nantes, France
860	Vikings attack Constantinople
865	Arrival of a large Viking army in England
866	York is captured by a Viking army
870s	Start of mass Viking settlement of Iceland
911	Normandy becomes a Viking territory under King Rollo
c.950	Ibrahim Al-Tartushi visits Hedeby in Denmark
954	The last Viking king of Jorvik is thrown out of York
c.982	Erik the Red sails to Greenland. Start of Viking settlements in Greenland
980s and 990s	New Viking attacks on England
c.1000	Leif Eriksson sails to North America and names it Vinland
1016	Knut becomes King of England
1042	Edward the Confessor becomes king of England
1066	Norwegian king Harald Hadrada is defeated at the Battle of Stamford Bridge. English king Harold II is defeated at the Battle of Hastings. William the Conqueror takes control of England
1080s	Final unsuccessful Viking attacks bring the Viking Age to a close in England
1241	Snorri Sturluson is killed at Reykholt, Iceland

Glossary

antler one of the branched horns found on the head of an adult deer

archaeologist a researcher who studies the remains of ancient peoples and civilisations

byre a barn

chieftain a leader

colonize to settle in a place

colony a place under the control of another country and settled by people from that country

commerce trade

cottongrass a plant that grows in wet, boggy places which has a flower that looks rather like cotton wool

dowry money or property brought by a woman into a marriage

falcon a fast-flying bird that catches other small birds and animals as its prey

fertile soil that is fertile is able to produce lots of plants or crops

feud a long and bitter argument or dispute

fjord a long and narrow sea inlet between high mountains. Fjords are a feature of the landscape in Norway

fleece the wool coat of a sheep

forge a workshop where metal is heated and shaped into objects

herb a plant that can be used for medicine, flavouring or making perfume

livestock domestic animals such as cows, pigs or sheep

longhouse the main building of a Viking farm

loom a frame on which thread is woven into fabric

midden a rubbish tip

monastery a place where monks live and worship

myth an old story, often about gods, heroes or the histories of ancient peoples

Old Norse the language spoken by the Scandinavians during Viking times

plunder to steal goods forcibly

raider someone who makes a surprise attack and takes loot

rampart a defensive wall

saga a long tale of heroic achievements, usually in Old Norse or Old Icelandic

sickle a farm tool with a semicircular blade, used for cutting crops or grass

skyr a dairy product made by the Vikings which is rather like yoghurt or soft cheese

thrall a slave

turf grass and the layer of soil that is held in its roots

volcanic describes the activity of volcanoes. Iceland lies in a region of great volcanic activity, where hot rock lies just beneath the surface of the ground

Index

archaeologists 7, 13, 25

bathing 7, 15
building materials 8, 9, 12

clothes 18, 19
cooking 11, 18, 22, 23, 24
craftworkers 24, 25
crops 20, 21, 22, 23, 24

Denmark 6, 7, 12, 23

families 16, 17
farms 6, 7, 8, 10, 16, 17, 18, 19, 20, 21, 22,
  23, 24
forges 11, 24, 25
furniture 14, 15

games 22, 27

houses 8, 9, 13, 14, 15, 16

Iceland 9, 15, 16, 19, 20, 27

livestock 10, 20
longhouses 8, 10, 11, 14, 15, 20

medicines 18

Norway 6, 7, 12, 19, 20, 23

raiding 7, 12, 16, 17
ramparts 12
rivers 7, 12

servants 17, 18
settlements 7, 12, 24
ships 12, 19
sport 27
Sturluson, Snorri 7
Sweden 6, 7, 12

thralls 17, 18
towns 9, 12, 13
trade 6, 12, 25

weaving 19

Resources

History from Objects: The Vikings, Colin Malam, Wayland 2010
All about Ancient Peoples: The Vikings, Anita Ganeri, Watts, 2009
Men, Women and Children in Viking Times, Colin Hynson, Wayland, 2009

http://www.jorvik-viking-centre.co.uk/
Website of the Jorvik Viking Centre in York
http://www.bbc.co.uk/schools/primaryhistory/vikings/
BBC site for children about the Vikings
http://www.foteviken.se/engelsk/indexe.htm/
Website about the Viking buildings at the Viking Reserve of Foteviken, Sweden